POSTCARDS · FROM ·

Mexico

Helen Arnold

RSVP
RAINTREE
STECK-VAUGHN
P U B L I S H E R S
The Steck-Vaughn Company

Austin, Texas

Published by Raintree Steck-Vaughn Publishers, an imprint of Steck-Vaughn Company

A ZOË BOOK

Editor: Kath Davies, Helene Resky
Design: Jan Sterling, Sterling Associates
Map: Gecko Limited
Production: Grahame Griffiths

Library of Congress Cataloging-in-Publication Data

Arnold, Helen.
    Mexico / Helen Arnold.
        p. cm. — (Postcards from)
    "A Zoë Book" — T.p. verso.
    Includes index.
    ISBN 0-8172-4012-8 (lib. binding)
    ISBN 0-8172-4233-3 (softcover)
    1. Mexico — Description of travel — Juvenile literature.
I. Title. II. Series.
F1216.5.A76 1996
972–dc20   95–7595
                                                                      CIP

Printed and bound in the United States
1 2 3 4 5 6 7 8 9 0 WZ 99 98 97 96 95

Photographic acknowledgments

The publishers wish to acknowledge, with thanks, the following photographic sources:

The Hutchison Library / Liba Taylor 22; Robert Harding Picture Library 24; South American Pictures / Tony Morrison - cover bl & r, title page, 6, 8, 10, 12, 14, 18, 20, 26, 28; / Robert Francis - cover tl; / Kimball Morrison 16.

The publishers have made every effort to trace the copyright holders, but if they have inadvertently overlooked any, they will be pleased to make the necessary arrangement at the first opportunity.

Contents

All the words that appear in **bold** are explained in the Glossary on page 30.

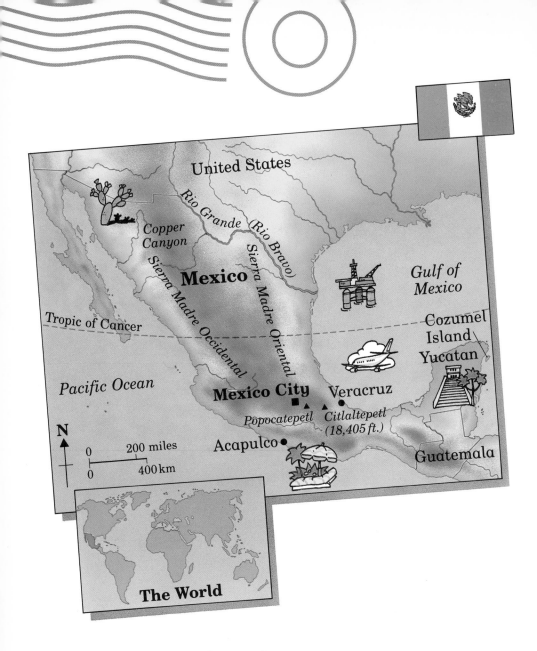

A big map of Mexico
and a small map of the world

Dear Liz,

You can see Mexico in red on the small map. It is below the United States. We flew here across the country. Mexico is three times the size of Texas.

Love,

Sarah

P.S. It took about 4 hours to fly here from Chicago. Mom says that the plane flew south across the United States.

A bird's eye view of Mexico City

Dear Paul,

This is Mexico City, the **capital** of Mexico. It is the biggest city in the world. This picture was taken from a high building. There are lots of them here.

Your friend,

Tim

P.S. Dad says that the air in the city is **polluted** because of all the cars. We travel on the **subway** to get away from all the traffic.

Eating out in Mexico City

Dear Tony,

Now I know where *tacos* and *tortillas* come from! People called **Aztecs** lived here long ago. They made a hot and tasty food called *tacos*. Then Spanish people came to live in Mexico. They made *tortillas*.

Your friend,

Robert

P.S. Mom told me that *tortillas* are Spanish pancakes. They are made of corn. *Tacos* are filled with meat and vegetables.

A stand in a craft market

Dear Jan,

Dad gave me some Mexican money called *pesos*. I bought a painted wooden fish in the market. The sun is very hot. Some people here wear great big hats called *sombreros*.

See you soon,

Ken

P.S. Dad says that Mexico is hot because it is in the **tropics**. It is cooler in Mexico City because it is high up in the mountains.

Two of the highest volcanoes in Mexico

Dear Jim,

We could see the tops of these **volcanoes** from Mexico City. They have very long names that I cannot spell. Most people here speak and write Spanish. Some people in the cities speak English, too.

Your friend,

Ray

P.S. Uncle Dan says that some **native** peoples in Mexico still speak the Aztec languages.

A train stops at Copper Canyon

Dear Ellie,

We came to Copper Canyon on the train. The **canyon** is very deep. People dug a metal called copper out of the rocks. Now you know why it is called Copper Canyon!

Love,

Janey

P.S. Mom says that people here ride horses and donkeys to get around. Animals are better than cars, because the roads are steep and rough in the mountains.

Divers at La Quebrada, Acapulco

Dear Alex,

We have just been swimming in the Pacific Ocean. We drove west through the mountains to get there. Can you see the divers? This is the most famous place on the ocean in Mexico.

Adios (that means Good-bye),

Pete

P.S. My friend says that there are monkeys and jaguars in the mountains near Acapulco. People are not allowed to hunt them, so the animals will not die out.

On the beach at Cozumel Island,
Yucatan, Mexico

Dear Joanna,

Now we are on the east coast of Mexico. American people like to come to the Gulf of Mexico for vacations. Mom wants to go **snorkeling**, so I am going to watch her.

Love,

Helen

P.S. Dad says that Mexico has two long coasts. It is cooler on the west coast by the Pacific Ocean. It rains more on the east coast by the Gulf of Mexico, but it is hotter!

The "Castle Pyramid" at Chichen Itza in the Yucatan, Mexico

Dear Jeff,

I thought the pyramids were in Egypt. There are some here in Mexico, too. They were built hundreds of years ago. There are 91 steps to the top of this pyramid.

Your friend,

Steve

P.S. Mom says that the **Mayan** people built this pyramid. They lived in Mexico long before the Aztecs. Some modern Mayan people still live in the Mexican **rain forests**.

Xochimilco, near Mexico City

Dear Rose,

We went for a trip on a boat like this one. It was covered in flowers. The boat went down a **canal** made by the Aztecs. The canal was built more than 500 years ago.

Love,

Gail

P.S. Dad says that children here start school when they are six. They learn about Mexico and the peoples who lived here in the past. They must have a lot to learn!

Playing volleyball in the park

Dear Sumeira,

We watched children playing this game. They were very fast. Mexican people are good at lots of sports. They swim and play soccer. Some of them ride horses in shows called *rodeos*.

Love from,

Taliah

P.S. My brother says that people who live in Mexico are lucky. The Olympic Games have been held here twice.

A festival in Mexico City

Dear Ralph,

People here love to dress up for special days, or **festivals**. They call them *fiestas*. These festivals are held all over Mexico. They often end with fireworks.

Sincerely,

Nat

P.S. Mom says that most people in Mexico are **Christians**. At *fiestas* they remember special Christians from the past.

The Mexican flag, flying in the
main square, Mexico City

Dear Justin,

I bought a little Mexican flag for you. The pictures on the flag come from Aztec times. They stand for the Aztec capital city. It was called Tenochtitlan.

Yours truly,

Tom

P.S. Dad says that the Spanish built Mexico City over the remains of Tenochtitlan. Mexico is not ruled by the Spanish now. Mexican people choose their own leaders. Mexico is a **democracy**.

Glossary

Aztecs: The peoples who ruled Mexico when the Spanish first came to the country

Canal: A river made by people

Canyon: A deep valley with steep sides

Capital: The town or city where people who rule the country meet

Christians: People who follow the teachings of Jesus

Democracy: A country where all the people choose the leaders they want to run the country

Festival: A time when people celebrate something special or a special time of year

Mayans: A people who lived in Mexico about 1,500 years ago

Native: Someone who was born in or connected with a place by birth

Pollute: To make something dirty

P.S.: This stands for Post Script. A postscript is the part of a card or letter that is added at the end, after the person has signed it.

Rain forest: The warm lands that are covered by trees near the middle of the Earth

Snorkeling: Swimming underwater while breathing through a tube

Subway: A train that runs under the ground

Tropics: Hot lands near the middle of the Earth that lie on the map between the Tropic of Capricorn and the Tropic of Cancer

Volcano: A mountain containing rock from inside the Earth. The hot rock comes out through a hole at the top of the volcano.

Index